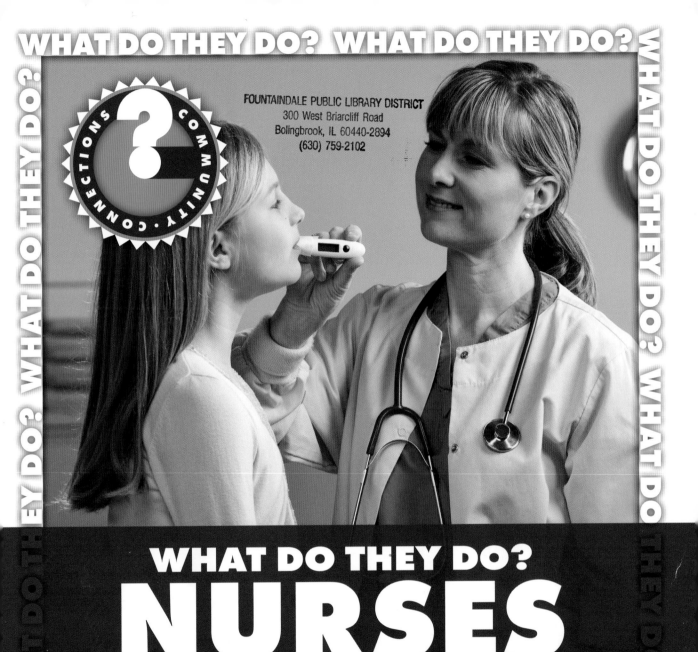

COMMUNITY · CONNECTIONS ?

# WHAT DO THEY DO?
# NURSES

BY JENNIFER ZEIGER

## CHERRY LAKE Publishing

Published in the United States of America by Cherry Lake Publishing
Ann Arbor, Michigan
www.cherrylakepublishing.com

Content Adviser: Kim Amer, PhD, RN, Associate Professor, DePaul University School of Nursing
Reading Adviser: Cecilia Minden-Cupp, PhD, Literacy Consultant

Photo Credits: Cover and page 1, ©AVAVA, used under license from Shutterstock, Inc.;
page 5, ©iStockphoto.com/LeggNet; page 7, ©iStockphoto.com/JSABBOTT; page 9,
©iStockphoto.com/nmaxfield; page 11, ©iStockphoto.com/monkeybusinessimages;
page 13, ©iStockphoto.com/DegasMM; page 15, ©iStockphoto.com/lisafx; pages 17 and 21,
©iStockphoto.com/sjlocke; page 19, ©Laurence Gough, used under license from Shutterstock, Inc.

**LIBRARY OF CONGRESS CATALOGING-IN-PUBLICATION DATA**
Zeiger, Jennifer.
  What do they do? Nurses / by Jennifer Zeiger.
    p. cm.—(Community connections)
  Includes bibliographical references and index.
  ISBN-13: 978-1-60279-808-3 (lib. bdg.)
  ISBN-10: 1-60279-808-7 (lib. bdg.)
  1. Nurses—Juvenile literature. 2. Nursing—Juvenile literature.
I. Title. II. Title: Nurses.
  RT82.Z45 2010
  610.73—dc22                          2009042804

Cherry Lake Publishing would like to acknowledge the
work of The Partnership for 21st Century Skills. Please
visit www.21stcenturyskills.org for more information.

Printed in the United States of America
Corporate Graphics Inc.
July 2010
CLFA07

NURSES

# CONTENTS

**WHAT DO THEY DO?**

# HELPING PEOPLE STAY HEALTHY

Have you ever visited a hospital or a doctor's office? Maybe you needed a checkup or were sick. Did you see a nurse? Nurses are there to help you. They help people feel better and stay healthy.

A nurse checks inside a person's ears.

Nurses work in hospitals and **clinics**. They spend time talking with **patients**. Nurses ask questions. They try to find out what is wrong. Nurses check a patient's heartbeat and **blood pressure**. They also take a patient's **temperature**. They teach people about eating good food and exercising.

Some nurses test their patients' blood.

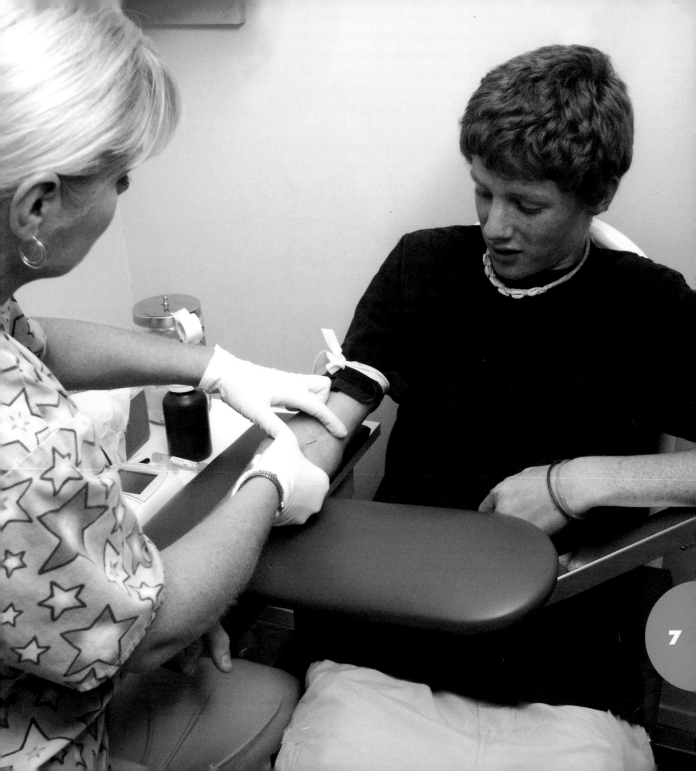

Nurses in hospitals make sure people get what they need. They check on each patient. They also give out **medicine**.

Sometimes, patients need extra care. They might need special tests. Nurses help run the tests. They also prepare patients for **operations**. They help people feel less scared and help their pain go away.

Nurses help doctors with operations.

Nurses often spend time around very sick people. How do nurses keep from getting sick themselves? One way is by always washing their hands. Can you think of other ways? Hint: Have you ever seen a nurse wearing a mask?

9

Nurses offer patients comfort and advice. They might explain how an illness will feel. Nurses also tell patients what to do when they go home. Nurses tell patients what to eat and when to take medicine.

A nurse can help a patient understand what will happen next.

# EVERY DAY AND EVERYWHERE

Hospitals need nurses every day. A nurse might work at night or on weekends. Nurses often work during holidays. Even though the work is hard, it feels good to help people.

Nurses keep files about their patients.

13

Not all nurses work in hospitals. Some visit people in their homes. Others work in schools or neighborhoods. Some work in doctor's offices. Many work for the army, navy, or air force. Nurses are experts who advise others about illness and health. Sometimes, the police ask nurses to help them solve crimes.

Some nurses visit patients at their homes.

Take a good look at a nurse's uniform. There are many different kinds. How are they alike? Do they have pockets? Look at the shoes. Do they look comfortable?

15

Some nurses learn to help a certain group of people. They might choose to work with children or new mothers. Some work with older people who need special care. A nurse might also help people who have a certain illness. For example, some nurses help patients who have **asthma**.

Some nurses work only with young patients.

# TEACHERS, ROLE MODELS, AND FRIENDS

Some nurses teach students who are studying to become nurses. They teach in classrooms or hospitals. Others teach the public. They might talk on television or the radio.

Nursing students learn about science and the human body.

Do you want to know more about being a nurse? Next time you see a nurse, ask questions. Why did he become a nurse? What does he like about his job? Maybe you'll get surprising answers!

19

Has the school nurse ever visited your classroom? She might have talked about keeping yourself healthy. She might also have tested your sight or hearing.

Nurses help people everyday. It isn't always easy work. We should be grateful that nurses are there when we need them!

Nurses use computers to keep track of patients.

# GLOSSARY

**asthma** (AZ-muh) a condition in which a person sometimes has difficulty breathing

**blood pressure** (BLUHD PRESH-ur) the force with which the blood presses against the walls of blood vessels, such as veins or arteries. Having high blood pressure can be unhealthy

**clinics** (KLIN-iks) places where people can go for medical treatment or advice

**medicine** (MED-uh-suhn) a drug used for treating sickness

**operations** (op-uh-RAY-shuhnz) procedures in which people's bodies are cut open to repair damaged parts or remove diseased parts

**patients** (PAY-shuntss) people who are receiving care from doctors, nurses, or other health professionals

**temperature** (TEM-per-uh-chur) a measure of heat or coldness. Having a high temperature often means a person is sick

# FIND OUT MORE

## BOOKS

Kenney, Karen Latchana. *Nurses at Work*. Edina, MN: Magic Wagon, 2010.

Minden, Cecilia, and Linda M. Armantrout. *Nurses*. Mankato, MN: The Child's World, 2006.

## WEB SITES

### KidsHealth
*kidshealth.org/kid/*
Learn all about staying healthy and how your body works.

### NJHA Kid's Career Corner
*www.njha.com/healthrecruitment/kid/*
Play games to learn more about nursing and other health careers.

# INDEX

## ABOUT THE AUTHOR

Jennifer Zeiger studied English at DePaul University. She now lives in the Chicago area with her two cats. She would like to thank nurses everywhere for working so hard to keep people healthy!

24